The Modern Copernicus

The Modern Copernicus

IAIN BAMFORTH

1984
The Salamander Press
EDINBURGH

The Salamander Press Edinburgh Ltd
34 Shandwick Place, Edinburgh EH2 4RT

ISBN 0 907540 49 X (cloth)
ISBN 0 907540 48 1 (paper)

First published 1984

*The publisher acknowledges
financial subsidy from the Scottish Arts Council
towards the publication of this volume*

Printed and made in Great Britain.
Set in Monotype Caslon by Speedspools, Edinburgh.
Printed by The Black Pennell Press, Greenock
on Salamander 'Requiem' long life laid paper
made by William Sommerville & Son plc.
Bound by Hunter & Foulis Ltd.
Designed by Tom Fenton at the Salamander Press.

Acknowledgements

Some of these poems have appeared previously in *Agenda*, *Cencrastus*, *Glasgow University Magazine*, *The E. C. Gregory Anthology 1983*, *Honest Ulsterman*, *Kenyon Review* (U.S.A.), *Lines Review*, *Literary Review*, *New Edinburgh Review*, *P.N. Review*, *Scottish Review*.

Particular debt is due to *The Poems of Li Ho* (J. D. Frodsham, Oxford, 1970); and to the Scottish Arts Council for a bursary in 1982 which made the completion of this volume possible.

Contents

Flowers Considered as Gestures *page* 11
The Modern Copernicus 12
The Idiot 13
The Dialogue of Anguish and Desire 14
De Signatura Rerum 19
A Little Requiem 21
Agony in the Garden 22
The Troublesome Reign 24
Love in Another Language 25
Letters from the T'ang 26
1. Mowing Grass and Setting Our Nets 28
2. Blue Houses 29
3. An Ancient Arrowhead from the Battlefield 30
4. The Screen 32
5. New Bamboo Shoots in my North Garden 33
Walking Back to China 34
The Tempest 38
Goethe's Last Night in Italy 40
In an Etruscan Dialect 41
The Magi 42
The Art of Fugue 45
Light Inseparable from Its Setting 47

When they saw the star, they rejoiced with exceeding great joy.

Amicum-philosophum de melancholia

Anything becomes interesting if you look at it long enough.
GUSTAVE FLAUBERT

Flowers Considered as Gestures

Their scents endure the earth, beheaded flowers
Threading water to their stalks and bowing
In fallen postures of the dead. Colours
Are their fading. Each act and suffering
Finds perfect form in them, that multitude
So vivid in its solitude. They take,
From each brief severance and attitude
Of death, the colours that their gestures make.

The Modern Copernicus

'Let therefore this little Mathematitian,
dread Emperour, withdraw himselfe to his owne company'

JOHN DONNE
Ignatius His Conclave 1611

I have stood still, and watched the world pass by
Through such a dream of history the mad
Might calm, and Christ, in his abandonment,
Be reconciled to this attending earth
Where meteor-showers and stars are calendars
And stillness is an ecstasy of flight
Which wakes me, like a child, towards that last
Strange burning of the dead, burnt-offerings
Blazing nocturnally against the light,
Epiphanies made choice and succulent
And featureless. So I once thought myself,
Deceived by balms, acquainted with the night;
Familiar with those dead and dispossessed
And those blurred, far-fetched colours of the mind
Whose shallow truths have perjured easily
To verge on Paradise, that best of worlds
Where I stand still, and watch the world pass by
Though all that moved me once has come to rest.

The Idiot

Beneath his moons it is a brazen god,
A god of shades and underworlds, who bids me come
To his abysmal sanctuary and spoiled epiphany
And this hermaphroditic, charmed debauch ;
Rises, imponderably, with infinite disdain
To celebrate his marriage with the air
And mock a virgin's prayer become voluptuary
Or floridly, a surfeited nostalgia.

The dead smile lately in their gauzy wraps ;
Envy such luminescent colours of the sun
Fleshing the asphodels with wormy leaves.
I hymn his bawdy queen with lutanists
And plague him with such lewd idolatry
His sycophantic court seems reticent ;
Or blandish consolations with indulgent ease
In aureate modes, as postured as the dead.

His helot fool, I maunder through the wastes
Bringing intact chaste tokens of his love.
I choose the species of that bestiary
Sphinx-like and fabulous ; displaying such largesse
To spoil his rage with falser sentiments
Than those a mock humanity bequeaths to fools
And vast Assyrians. Those beasts will eat
My heart as I, so prodigally, eat ashes too.

The Dialogue of Anguish and Desire

'Neither entirely guilty
nor altogether innocent'
RACINE

I

Nightbirds, a windfall of charred leaves:
Your cold lips search me in the dark

Where nothing sings or comes to light.
That love has made us desolate.

II

We suffer both the same harsh god.
His fatigued angels weigh on us,

Proceeding elsewhere to their stars.
(How can we love, not knowing death?)

III

Beneath these calm and formal skies
Where you grow old, and I distraught,

A candle sometimes burns at night
To plunder god of pallid stars.

IV

The stars, above us, are at war :
They burn our eyes, or fall to earth

Where what we knew as provenance
Blows ashen, gathered for the winds.

V

Sunlight discolours in its lamps :
I cannot sleep when you are gone

And nothing here resembles you.
Needing no god, our god is here.

VI

The birds are still, in other worlds :
That sleepless land deceives us both

With apprehended, glittering stars,
And this, a place left for the dead.

VII

You talk in sleep, and dream sometimes
Of stars at war, unearthly lights

Where all our grief is meaningless.
That hope is anguish and desire.

VIII

A light blows earthwards from the stars
And we take arms for all the dead

Made desolate, like us, through love.
Their laughter mingles with the leaves.

IX

Loved or endured, the day is gone,
And birds have fled their anguished song:

Night after night, you hold the lamp
To fire the coffers of the dead.

X

The lamps grow dimmer on the earth.
Sometimes I apprehend those stars

In formal songs, cold stratagems
Of love and war. Then come the snows.

XI

Though you have dreamed so urgently
That god descends from his machine

And takes these painted cloths for dreams;
He feigns his joys, and does not love.

XII

Why touch me now, why make me sad?
We watch here nightly for the dead

While all around the waters grow
And trees blow clear of all their snow.

XIII

Frail stars have fallen from the sky
And left their gestures in the air.

In time of war, that night will pass
And love redeem what is not love.

XIV

What shall we call that other day
Where we keep watch, and join those prayers

Whose love has made us desolate
Hymning the dead, who are not sad . . .

De Signatura Rerum

Apocalypsis cum figuris

Just when the woodcut splits across its length
And sunlight flames his tarred and feathered wings
He falls, through all his senses, to the world.
That lightning cleaves the earth and rents the sky

And rains upon cracked mortar and loose tiles,
Leaving this Gothic air quite still and cold ;
The phoenix-eggs and lodestones, magic squares,
Those pyramids of texts and shards of Christ

All scattered in the corners of the room.
Some God he taught to speak with blasphemies
Has galled Creation with a scroll of worms,
A Zeitgeist, meteor-showered and weirdly lit,

Where, lost in love and love's extremities
And half-asleep beneath these makeshift Alps,
Casting the eye-motes from the Judgement Day
The damned evacuate their common ground.

Though Europe looms with rumours of itself
The sanctified are stiff with holiness :
Those shadow-clouds and highest atmospheres,
A purest force of stars, so chars the air

That hymnbooks, algebras, celestial globes,
Those faint votive-lights of the sacrament,
Have spawned in this millenial Dürer-scene
A man who counterfeits his Judgement Day

And contemplates such perfect artifice
That God must bend before the harvest-tide,
A weathered continent give up its dead
That he might chart his plummet to the sea.

What daylight silhouettes across the Rhine
Commends the dead to nothing more than sleep,
A futile art still gleaned among its shards
With some dry hourglass and an abstract fear,

Chance residues, and mock Ash-Wednesdays.
That old woodcut engraved with many prayers
Confounds its patrons with obscurities ;
And some mistake the lightning for a storm

To arc the rainbow over this cursed earth.
Just when the woodcut split across its length
And sunlight flamed his tarred and feathered wings
He fell, through all his senses, to the world.

A Little Requiem
1756-1791

Disturbed by your silence, I dream a world
As simple as the song that guides me here,
And sleep, my eyes wide open to the dark.
I find nowhere on earth to mark your grave.

That they might reconcile me to that time
The creatures of your cortège follow me
Where stillness is an uproar of the birds . . .
Clap with delight and they all disappear !

Agony in the Garden

Once more they beg me to begin again.
An old waterwheel creaks through the night
And a handful of birds set fire to the sky.
Here in the garden I hold my breath.

I come too late to know the mysteries
Coiling round this untransfigured tree;
And when I wonder what strange blood
Congeals as savagely as mine—

How miracles of fish and loaves
Could find an origin beneath the self-same skies
That heralded some ordinary birth
Among the customary beasts

And fruitless nights of prayer
Still guide the wisest men in worship
To a dumb child-king—
That too-much-travelled innocence

Within a wholly different world
So circumscribes the nature of my agony.
A withered cypress-tree still shivers in the heat
To mock this sufferance of doubt;

And blind, devoted Judas stalks
Through all of Peter's sea-fleshed dreams,
Remaining at a distance from the tree
Devised so long ago in Bethlehem,

Where Magdalene, dry-eyed with pieties,
And never so estranged from this familiar death,
Has swaddle-clothed my limbs for other balms
Than those of frankincense and myrrh ;

As if that indiscreet embrace
And slighter miracle of bread and wine
Redeems the kings, come walking on the waves
To reach Gathsemane before the evening sets

And they betray themselves a second time.
I watch while that faint light of day
Breaks in the east, falters as it came.
My mother, weeping, stoops beneath her years

And lays me strangely in the shroud.
Those gaudy effigies of angels fall to earth
And all Creation parodies itself.
Here in the garden I sham my death.

The Troublesome Reign

I'm the true king of the rain-provinces,
Surveyor of all countries to the seas ;
A charmed usurper—jejune but merciless—
Impatient, waiting for the rains to cease.

Though envoys never reach this frontier-world
All tributes crown the thorns of my disdain :
Subdued by famines and a necessary war
My people fall in thousands when it rains.

I'm tired of pallid lives yoked to my laws,
A peepshow gossip and a court's requests ;
My alchemists, whose dross is always dross,
The spoon-fed sycophancies of my guests.

Le Roi s'Amuse !—tired of my falcons' spleen
And father's book-of-hours and fleur-de-lys,
I waste no time with homesick courtesans ;
Pretenders, strung on gibbets by the sea.

Hermaphrodites, barbarians, pariahs—
I'm weary of every tawdry aspect of myself ;
Those stylised, twittering birds of paradise
No less convention than this reign itself.

Court no longer fawns attendance on my word.
Those halcyon days are Dog-starred ; this legacy
Befouled by rabble. There I strut, an awkward
Buffoon, mocking all men with their society.

Love in Another Language

I

There is no healing touch in mine,
A studied Lazarus with the gift of tongues
Whose word is all it cannot be.

II

The stuttered cadence of my love
Relives its strangeness in the commonplace,
Betrayed into that Purgatory.

III

A merciless routine of days . . .
How much I would caress your long-lost words
To wake beyond their provenance.

IV

The metaphor translates itself
From necessary and circumstantial pains :
Its tongue becomes my sacrament.

Letters from the T'ang

(from the Chinese of Li Ho)

1. *Mowing Grass and Setting Our Nets*

With your patterned tail-coat
And so finely feathered brocade
How you strut across the fields
To feed your fledglings !

To the east ripe grain lies flattened
By the harvest winds ;
Don't listen to the decoy
East of the dike.

The men of Ch'i have woven nets
As transparent as air :
They string them out across each field
Unlevelled by the reapers.

Those silken nets drape everywhere
And throw no shadows—
Run foul of them and your head
Will bloody your coat.

Who gathered this florid camouflage
Of moxa leaves ?
You cannot guess at the deception
Hidden within . . .

2. *Blue Houses*

My home is in Heng-t'ang
Where red sendal curtains billow with cassia.
I have piled up my hair
In dark-blue clouds
And the moons have become
Pearls for my ears.

This spring by the river
The wind bends water-reeds.
Far away in the south
They detain northerners.
You, my lord, eat scraps from their tables—
I suffer the delicacies.

Please don't show me
The way to Hsiang-yang!
Few sails ever return
From that overgrown reach of the river.
A withered tree there
Confuses the water-reeds.

3. *An Ancient Arrowhead from the Battlefield*

Lacquer dust and powdered bone
And red-streaked cinnabar :
Their old-men's blood gushed out
To bear these bronze flowers.
The white feathers and gilt shaft
Have rotted in the rain—
Only the three broken wolf's-teeth
Of the spine remain.

With my two tired horses
I searched east of the post-station
Where Ch'ang-p'ing is choked with stones
And the plain overgrown with weeds.
Some tattered clouds passed by
And soon the day crept to its end :
Beneath each desolate star
I was abandoned to the dark.

On every side the dead
Shrieked out their wasted flesh.
I drained some curds from my flask
And offered charred meat as victual.
But the insects were silent, the geese
Swooned from reed-shoots blighted long ago.
Their voices flickered in the fire ;
Pursued me when I fled.

I sought this place in vain
And found only a broken arrow
Whose shattered point, rusted and snapped,
Once pierced through human flesh.
In the eastern quarter, travelling south,
A young pedlar on horseback
Urged me to exchange the relic
For a votive-basket.

4. *The Screen*

With its hinges of silver
And butterflies falling on China pinks,
Its duck-head green and frozen water
And glass-coin fastenings,
The twelve folds hide a lamp
Smouldering orchid-oil.
She lets down her hair before the mirror
And sheds her gold cicada hairpin :
A purplish aloes-smoke
Mingles with dogwood.
Their wine-glasses are tied
With a bridal sash ;
Outside the wind scatters dew,
Moonlight glints on the screen
And birds cry from the city walls—
The girl from Ch'u sleeps on.

5. *New Bamboo Shoots in my North Garden*

The bamboo-skin sloughs from the lengthening shoots
Leaving a peeled skin of jade.
In a single night it is completely grown—
Soaring a thousand feet from its roots
In the mud by the garden pool.

* * *

I have cut down green bamboos to write my verses.
Over the perfumed oils and spring powder
Scrawl these bitter, passionless words.
Who will see them?—weighed down by the dew,
Mourning their branches fading in the mist.

* * *

By the family-well two or three shoots have poked
Through gaps in the flagstones:
At dawn I noticed their roots hidden by the path.
Next spring, when the waters rush across the sands
I'll strip away the jade and make fishing-rods.

* * *

Like Mao-ling, I've come home to exult in poverty.
Ancient bamboos torment the clouds with their years!
The wind blows and the shoots bend in the rain,
And nightjars perch on one stem whose shadow
Stoops, almost, into my wine-glass.

Walking Back to China

I

Here, at the frontier, there are leaves
And brittle frosts, and the long days.
So do not ask what time of year
The birds shower south from the Steppes
To a slow death, and these dog days.
Tell me when they leave, or return.

II

Though you recall me in that land
From which the birds return in spring
And I do not, how will you know
When all resemblance ends, dreaming
This world in silence to yourself—
A mere pretence from journeying?

III

How often I have thought of home
Beneath strange roofs, while all night long
It rained, and all the seasons passed.
Elsewhere, ships freeze in the cold sea
And there is scarcely light enough
To read, or walk back to China.

IV

Your voice fades when you call.
Knowing the postures of the dead
And places that a thought might grow
Tell me, how is silence there—
That sounds so hollow in my voice
With tales of new atrocities?

V

Fresh winds have shed the cypress-trees
And sunlight, shifting through the clocks,
Seems ashen, gathered in the hearth,
To mock such auguries and prayers
Whose loves, I practise carelessly.
I close my eyes and sleep at night.

VI

Then, when I crossed the frontier-post
I learned that there were sufferings too;
That plagues, the annual massacres
Were feast-days for the Emperor
And penance for his courtesans.
What have I done there but desire?

VII

Spring is coming. A gentle wind
Is tearing blossom from the trees
Though thousands will die when they bloom.
Sometimes, drunk with fatigue, I dream
Of those rare, cultivated flowers
That will not last the journey home.

VIII

A harsh light drifts across the stalks
And all my nights are full of ghosts
And dynasties, and those blown husks
Of the T'ang. I have learnt patience,
And the whims of an old, barbarous king
To stay young in his capital.

IX

There are whispers and introductions.
After a while, you cease listening
And watch the gaudy Chinese lanterns
Swaying in the wind until it rains.
Why is it then, you wake at night
And search for me with such disquiet?

X

Why the lamp—the day is breaking
And what is distance to you now—
So far from wars and massacres?
Nightjars migrate to nest the land
And seaweed, gathering with your dreams,
Becomes charred driftwood on the shore.

XI

When I am old, and near my death
And cannot speak my mother-tongue,
When daylight fades these billet-doux
And silence clamours from your lute,
Where will the frontiers shift in sleep
And come close, even for a time.

XII

You say, you say; and you forget
Those slaughtered birds and lengthening dreams
Which hold no colour but their own.
I marvel at the falling snow
And learn the science of farewells—
What have I done there but desire?

The Tempest

'And my ending is despair'

Venice does not mend. This Christmas,
A hundred churches' wintered bells
Will celebrate somewhere at sea
Those dead across the continent
Still born and swallowed up in Christ.
Hosannahs swell above the flood.
Rain-pocked, decayed, the Saviour's head
Slumps down upon his wooden chest
And peers towards Murano's spires ;
His cross-beamed tree is everywhere
And everywhere the candles drift
As though a wind had caught the hair
Of comets, dragged them down to earth
As lightning-tear and wound for all
Whose artistry is world enough
To gain a tinselled crown of thorns.

Beneath Byzantine monuments
And whispering dry Palladian domes
Those mannered men are circumspect ;
Their Christ composed, they muse sometimes
And bend before their holly-trees
To ponder on each token gift,
Begging a blessing for the State
Whose waves are scrolled upon the sea.
No dead leaves here can spoil the view
To San Michele's unstoned graves
That line above the high-tide gates
And open-mouthed, gaze out to sea ;

That sea grows old in stunned repose
And shelters in its grand Canals
From sea-squalls, Behemoths, and wars.
But Venice, craftless, creaks with tides,
And I, who would abjure its trade,
Have measured out the citadel
Whose firmament still seethes with stars
And sunlight, guttered on the stones.

This I knew once. There he grows old,
And now I watch the candles stray
In rows of almost-human forms
While far above the chill lagoon
They sear their comets through my eyes
To wound me with the tempest-tossed.
That much I doubt. The nation's spires
Still celebrate somewhere at sea
A child whose tears have drowned the world
And saved us in our Jonas-shoals.
He will not wed my Doges' ring.
This Christmas, when I would appease
That guileless head fleshed with thorns
He bends in mourning for the world
Where he, at length, has come to rest.
My Lord is broken in his bread.

Goethe's Last Night in Italy

The gods, visibly absent, haunt themselves
In bronze ; unearthed to the known world
From the tragic haze of marginal heliotropes
And asphodels. Grief makes them older
Than their years, sun-drenched in the tombs,
Plagued by nightingales and some vain,
Elusive thought a watercolourist would purify.
Thus Venus—risen from her scallop-shell—
Might gesture prepubescent Eros to her side
And a solitary Judas-tree bend with fruit
To cradle its incredulous miracle. Tonight,
Tapping the rain-gauge's caged barometer,
I wonder at those strange Renaissance songs
And lachrimae, and the more gentle holocaust
Of the renounced Penates, serene to this mute
Abandonment and consecration as necessity.
Absolved from their autumnal passing-on,
This last barbarian journeys to the classic
End of day ; his sentimental education
Brought to the Alps, unburdened with gestures
Or the muddled human dreams so many gods
Confuse with immortality, fond indifference
With a poor-man's nervous-tic of irony.

In an Etruscan Dialect

Forgive me for what
I would take from you
And for the nothing I replace,
For reconciling you at last
To the shades.

Forgive me for leaving
Each god beyond the threshold,
For taking your dead face in my hands
And uttering these healing words
I cannot believe.

Forgive me for loving
The darkness in your eyes,
For seeking distance to bring together
All that holds me forever
Unapproachable.

Forgive me for speaking
In this Etruscan dialect,
For the useless dressing of the dead
And this indecipherable stone,
Left for the journey.

The Magi

'Come l'uom s'eterna . . .'

I

Their hands drip myrrh, and practise miracles
Despite the indiscretions of the dead
And freshly crucified. All pasts become
Their past, a wilderness of childish rhymes
Whose promised land of lunar permanence
Some cultivate as home. In Samarkand
Each wakes, beneath the same, unworldly sun
Which he, through self-regard, would turn to gold.

II

Few, dug from their sick-beds, are brought alive
To witness this last flowering of the earth
Yielding, through them, its fruit—resemblances
That spawn unnoticed in the temperate zones.
They pity none but those serenely damned
Defected from the tomb, dazed by a star.
The Christ-child, long outnumbered by the dead,
Is heaven-sent, with nothing much to say.

III

The meteors fall, sublimely, through their palms.
Made ready to depart, they brood on hope
That mitigates so much its own terrain
And half-deceives, with common sufferings,
A far-fetched age. Thus some, in their domain
Are damned, but seem the last presumptive blessed.
Anonymous, the dead maintain that ground;
Are set apart in proximate embrace.

IV

The rare, pale sun of their nostalgia
Grows bright; survives a cruder currency
Scoured clean and washed, and still convertible.
Some, empty-handedly, count their blessings—
Knowing those dreaming and long-dead are blind
To prompt disasters and chill holocausts.
From such charred vestiges their prayer-wheels glean
A blurred, exquisite light; blown from the stars.

V

Their eyes are wet with rain. They are estranged;
But eloquent, each in his way, of love:
Enduring nothing but dumb paradigms
That they, unanswerably, must apprehend.
So they dispose themselves, through loss and gain,
In shallow graves. For them, compassion breeds
Its pieties and troubled worldliness,
A passion-song in lieu of Paradise.

VI

Despite this permanence of flared sun-spots
And alien consciences, their miracles
Are burdened with that pure, peremptory star
Which costs the earth. Beyond the Caucasus
Frail kings might grasp its price of innocence—
Appalled by refugees and Auschwitz-scenes
And travellers in hieratic, dimmed distress :
This, the long-sought blessing, they cannot bless.

VII

They are not here. The ash-pits freeze ; the dead,
Subdued beneath a wilderness of names,
Have witness only through the witness-blind
To resurrect day-stars. The civilised,
Despite their discontents, bow down in prayer :
Nothing is left for providence to save
But this, some other way of standing still.
The Second Coming, almost, is at hand.

VIII

Under that fragile, contemplated sun
A brief, persistent death has come to light.
This is the turning of its will—nothing
Resembles less those retinued dream-beasts
And spent spikenards. Each coffer fills with rain.
So they presume to tell us where they are.
Elsewhere, from time to time, a comet flares
And falls remotely over humankind.

The Art of Fugue

'I describe not the essence but the passage'
MONTAIGNE

In these last, furtive days of the empire,
Like any other fugitive I wake uneasily at night,
And watch the meteors showering incandescently
Above their own decay ; endure the tyrannies
And those intimidating Northern Lights,
A history made poetry, a residue of tears
Refined until the damned cry out their innocence
And some old man comes home, sleepwalking
From the wars, and does not speak, but stares
So fondly at the household gods and patron-saints
Grown fat and Buddha-like above the hearth,
Dreaming of convalescence from their underworld
Into an altogether stranger circumstance
Where lepidopteries and catalogues of rare
Protected birds are all the rage. I cultivate
Such visions of eternity, apostrophised
In a flood of refugees, blind astrophores
Charting the martial progress of their star :
Though I would pray to some obscurer deity
Empty-handed, word-perfect, recalling the dead
To the distant fury of battle, a critical
Half-light, frenzied solitudes of weather-forms
Whose subterfuge of clouds and frontier-zones
Once seemed a habitable place where evergreens
Might bloom. So the lords of limit put an end
To all unbidden Siren-songs, and I have come,
At least, to know those dead, authentic men
Leading their senile fathers by the hand

Into the promised land, as if so many dead
Might civilise the earth, or find themselves
Among self-healing gods and blurred phenomena,
A wilderness made sweetly harsh and plentiful.
Those mad, migratory years are yours also :
The new ascendancy where I shall wake at night,
Prey to fugues and a pale, immaculate light
From my childhood years. Somewhere I drift
On that mania, a querulous frugality of sleep ;
Enduring these apocrypha and genealogies,
God's vagaries and a bleak, portentous climate
That proves synonymous the undiscerning dead.
Marvelling at the fossil-proofs of authenticity
And afterlights of grace, I render to the gods,
Lapsed in decrepitude, such paltry weathermarks,
Varied signs of abuse that might survive decay,
The coming-on of sleep in a critical sublime
And miraculous light, or this separate dark
Resonant with fugues, where stars, metamorphosed
And utterly banal, begin their fatal journey
Through a real terrain. I have far to walk
From that obscured frontier ; haunted to sleep
And numbed by the known world, like those first
Vainglorious predators of the Adoration.

Light Inseparable from Its Setting

Invoke my guilty
Shade with reticence
For untold random
Sorrows weeping dress
Their sullen lamps
In human attitude

As if the setting
Of archaic plenitude
Might be a suffering
Precisely resolute
Among such paradisal
Ironies of grief

Where some enduringly
Indifferent piety
Must lay a faithless
Shade again to rest
And bless its augured
Paucity of light